WNBA Hot Ticket

WASHINGTON MYSTICS

JOSH ANDERSON

To Leo and Dane, the biggest superstars I've ever met.

The stats and information in this book are accurate through the 2024 WNBA season.

Copyright © 2026 by Lerner Publishing Group, Inc.

All rights reserved. International copyright secured. No part of this book may be reproduced, stored in a retrieval system, or transmitted in any form or by any means—electronic, mechanical, photocopying, recording, or otherwise—without the prior written permission of Lerner Publishing Group, Inc., except for the inclusion of brief quotations in an acknowledged review.

Lerner Publications Company
An imprint of Lerner Publishing Group, Inc.
241 First Avenue North
Minneapolis, MN 55401 USA

For reading levels and more information, look up this title at www.lernerbooks.com.

Main body text set in Aptifer Slab LT Pro / Typeface provided by Linotype AG

Library of Congress Cataloging-in-Publication Data

Names: Anderson, Josh, author.
Title: Washington Mystics / Josh Anderson.
Description: Minneapolis : Lerner Publications, 2026. | Series: Lerner sports. WNBA hot ticket | Includes bibliographical references and index. | Audience: Ages 7–11 | Audience: Grades 2-3 | Summary: "The Washington Mystics have lost more games than they've won since joining the WNBA in 1998. In 2019, they put their past behind them and won the league championship. Explore the team and its players"—Provided by publisher.
Identifiers: LCCN 2024046202 (print) | LCCN 2024046203 (ebook) | ISBN 9798765670101 (library binding) | ISBN 9798765683583 (paperback) | ISBN 9798765682135 (epub)
Subjects: LCSH: Washington Mystics (Basketball team)—History—Juvenile literature.
Classification: LCC GV885.52.W39 A64 2026 (print) | LCC GV885.52.W39 (ebook) | DDC 796.323/6409797—dc23/eng/20241218

LC record available at https://lccn.loc.gov/2024046202
LC ebook record available at https://lccn.loc.gov/2024046203

Manufactured in the United States of America
1 – CG – 12/15/24

TABLE OF CONTENTS

FIVE MINUTES TO HISTORY 4

FACTS AT A GLANCE 5

CHAPTER 1
A TEAM IN THE US CAPITAL 9

CHAPTER 2
AMAZING STARS 15

CHAPTER 3
FINALLY THE FINALS. 21

CHAPTER 4
A NEW START 27

Glossary. 30
Learn More 31
Index 32

Washington Mystics forward Elena Delle Donne (*right*) dribbles around Connecticut Sun defender Alyssa Thomas (*left*) during the 2019 WNBA Finals.

FIVE MINUTES

FACTS AT A GLANCE

- The **WASHINGTON MYSTICS** joined the Women's National Basketball Association (WNBA) as an expansion team in 1998.

- The Mystics won the team's first **WNBA TITLE** in 2019.

- Mystics forward **ELENA DELLE DONNE** won the league's 2019 Most Valuable Player (MVP) award.

- Guard **ARIEL ATKINS** is the team's all-time leader in three-point baskets.

The 2019 WNBA season had less than six minutes remaining. The Washington Mystics had been the league's best team all year. They were tied 72–72 with the Connecticut Sun in Game 5 of the WNBA Finals.

Moments like these are often when the best players become legends. The 2019 WNBA MVP, Elena Delle Donne, is one of those players. Mystics guard Aerial Powers dribbled the ball down the court and passed it to Delle Donne. Delle Donne stood with her back to the basket, covered by a defender. Connecticut's Alyssa Thomas guarded her closely and would not let her turn.

Delle Donne faked a pass and then dribbled left. The Mystics star faked another move before spinning on her right foot to face the basket. Delle Donne jumped to shoot over her defender's outstretched arm and hit the shot. The basket gave the Mystics a 74–72 lead.

A few minutes later, with the Mystics up by four points, Delle Donne was in the same spot on the court. Once again, Thomas guarded her closely. But Delle Donne was able to get past Thomas a second time. She dribbled toward the basket and put up a short shot that rattled against the rim. When the ball fell through the net, it gave the Mystics a six-point lead.

The buzzer sounded a few moments later, and Delle Donne and the Mystics celebrated the team's first championship. Fans in Washington, DC, had waited more than 20 years for this moment. Their team had won the WNBA title!

Elena Delle Donne (*center*) scored 152 points during the 2019 playoffs.

Mystics players celebrate after winning the team's first title in 2019.

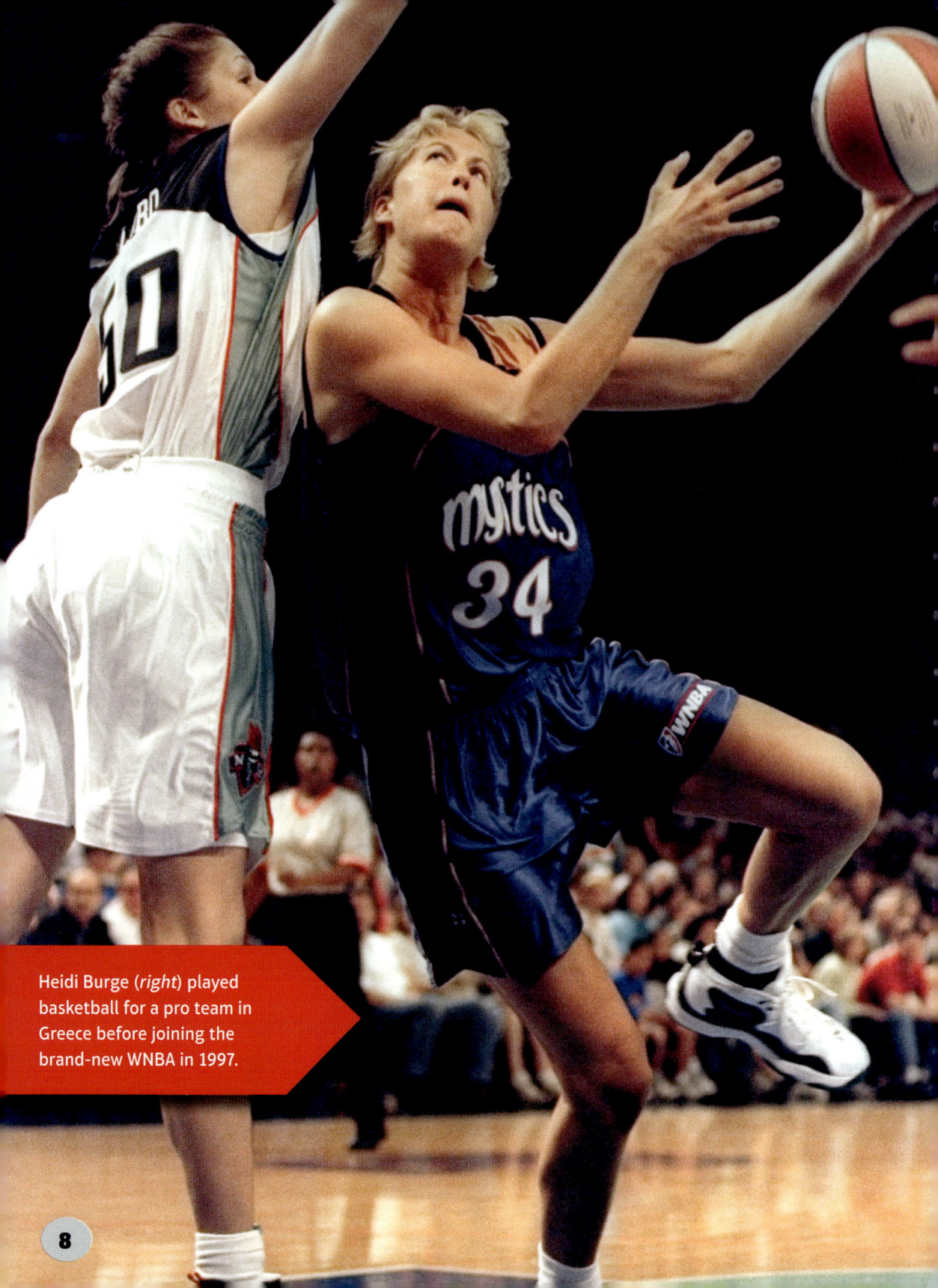

Heidi Burge (*right*) played basketball for a pro team in Greece before joining the brand-new WNBA in 1997.

CHAPTER 1
A TEAM IN THE US CAPITAL

The Washington Mystics started play during the WNBA's second season in 1998. Based in the US capital, Washington, DC, the Mystics were one of two expansion teams added to the league that year. The other was the Detroit Shock.

The Mystics are owned by the same group that owns the National Basketball Association's (NBA) Washington Wizards. Both teams' colors are red, navy blue, silver, and white. The Mystics play at the Entertainment and Sports Arena in Washington's Congress Heights neighborhood.

The team's colors honor the red, white, and blue of the US flag.

The Mystics' first season in the WNBA was challenging. They finished with a 3–27 record, the worst in the league. Because they finished so poorly in 1998, Washington picked first overall in the 1999 WNBA Draft. They chose University of Tennessee star forward Chamique Holdsclaw.

With Holdsclaw on the roster, the Mystics improved quickly. Holdsclaw played for the team for six seasons and led the Mystics to the playoffs three times. During one of those trips to the playoffs, the Mystics won their first playoff series. They defeated the Charlotte Sting in the first round.

Mystics guard Kristi Toliver (*left*) shoots over a defender during a 2019 game.

Chamique Holdsclaw (*center*) averaged 18.3 points and nine rebounds during her six seasons with the Mystics.

The Mystics had many good players during the team's first 20 seasons. Washington appeared in the playoffs often, but the team never made it to the WNBA Finals. That changed in 2018 when the Mystics finally reached the league's biggest stage. But the team's first trip to the Finals was disappointing. The Mystics lost three games in a row to the Seattle Storm.

Emma Meesseman played for several pro teams in Europe when she wasn't playing in the WNBA.

The next season, forward Emma Meesseman rejoined the team after sitting out the 2018 WNBA season so she could play in Belgium. The Mystics had the league's best record in 2019. It was their best chance yet for a WNBA title.

A key player all season, Meesseman raised her scoring average to almost 18 points per game in the Finals. She helped lead the Mystics to win their first title. Meesseman was the MVP of the 2019 Finals.

Since their 2019 title, the Mystics have been to the playoffs a few times, but they have not won a series. Delle Donne, the team's biggest star, left the Mystics in 2023. The team is working hard to build another title-winning roster.

DISTRICT OF CHANGE

The Mystics aim to help the Washington, DC, community through their District of Change campaign. District of Change focuses on making an impact in several different areas. The team wants to help with issues related to race and gender, LGBTQIA+ rights, and social and economic problems in the community. One project the team supports is trying to help Washington, DC, become the 51st state. Becoming a state would give the people of Washington a stronger voice in the US government.

Members of the Mystics and the NBA's Washington Wizards team up at a Black Lives Matter event.

HOOPS SCOOP

In 2010, three Mystics players played in the WNBA All-Star Game. They were Monique Currie, Lindsey Harding, and Crystal Langhorne.

Chamique Holdsclaw plays in a 2001 game against the Portland Fire.

CHAPTER 2
AMAZING STARS

The Mystics' first superstar was Chamique Holdsclaw. Holdsclaw was one of college basketball's most successful players before she joined the WNBA. At Tennessee, Holdsclaw helped the women's basketball team win three national titles. She won the College Player of the Year award twice.

The Mystics picked Holdsclaw first overall in the 1999 WNBA Draft. She was an All-Star player during her first five seasons in the league. She played six total seasons in Washington.

Mystics players walk back onto the court after a time-out during a 2008 game.

Alana Beard played the first six seasons of her WNBA career for the Mystics. The team picked Beard second overall in the 2004 WNBA Draft. She was one of the team's top scorers during her time in Washington.

Beard was very accurate on three-point shots. But her impact was just as strong on defense. Beard was in the top 10 for steals in nine of her 14 WNBA seasons. She ranks fourth all-time with 709 career steals. She was an All-Star and a member of the WNBA's All-Defensive Team four times during her time in Washington.

Alana Beard (*right*) muscles past the Indiana Fever's Ebony Hoffman to make a shot during a 2006 game.

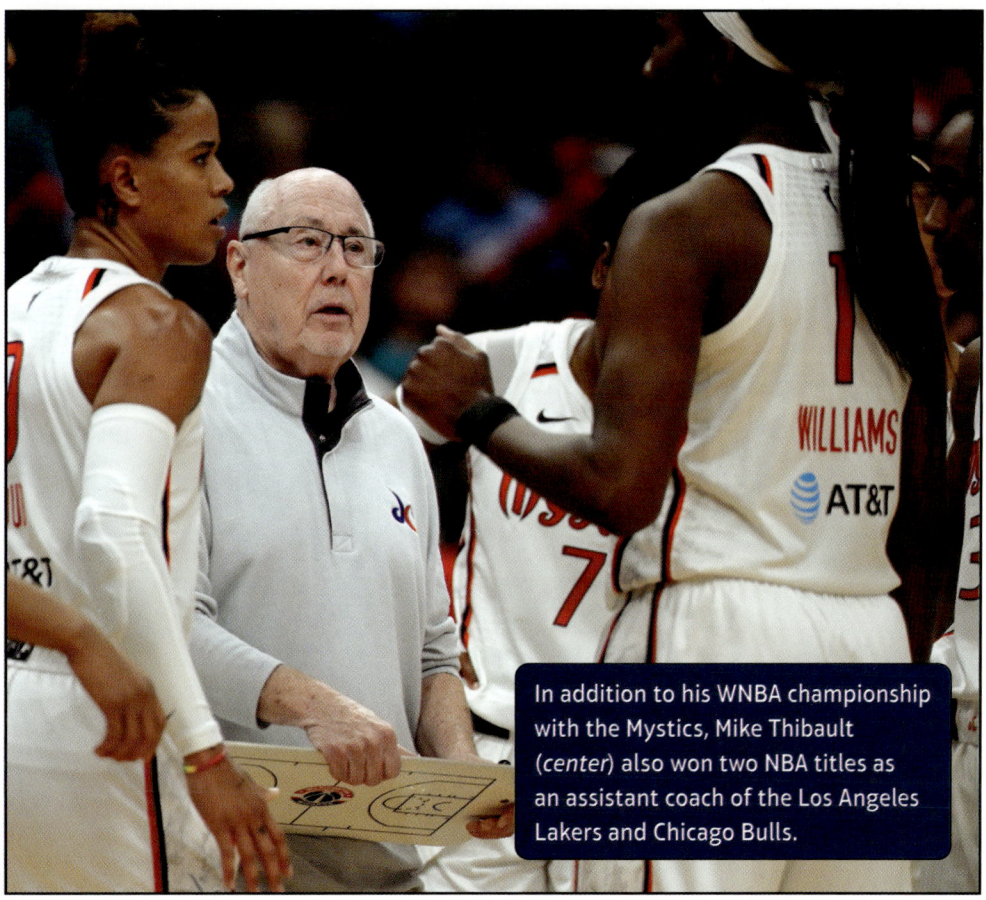

In addition to his WNBA championship with the Mystics, Mike Thibault (*center*) also won two NBA titles as an assistant coach of the Los Angeles Lakers and Chicago Bulls.

After coaching the Connecticut Sun for 10 years, head coach Mike Thibault took over as the Mystics' head coach in 2013. Thibault led the Mystics to the playoffs eight times. He coached Washington to a title in 2019. Thibault is the WNBA's all-time winningest coach with 379 wins. In 2022, he retired from coaching and became the team's general manager.

Playing in Washington from 2008 to 2013, Crystal Langhorne was one of the team's top players. Langhorne finished among the league's top 10 in rebounds four times and ranks 16th all-time in rebounding. Langhorne was an All-Star twice with the Mystics.

While Elena Delle Donne didn't start her career in Washington, she is among the very best players to wear a Mystics uniform. Before she joined the Mystics, Delle Donne played for the Chicago Sky. With the Sky, she won the Rookie of the Year award in 2013 and the league's MVP award in 2015.

A trade before the 2017 season brought Delle Donne to Washington. With the Mystics, Delle Donne earned four trips to the WNBA All-Star Game, won the 2019 MVP award, and led the team to the 2019 title. Delle Donne made more than 93 percent of her free throws. That's better than any other player in WNBA history. Her scoring average of 19.5 points per game ranks fifth all-time.

Elena Delle Donne made 142 free throws in 2017, which ranked fifth in the WNBA that season.

HOOPS SCOOP

Emma Meesseman's 193 career blocked shots are the most in team history.

Emma Meesseman (*right*) blocks a shot from the Atlanta Dream's Angel McCoughtry in a 2015 game.

During the 2018 WNBA playoffs, Elena Delle Donne (*left*) averaged a team-high 19.6 points and 9.5 rebounds per game.

CHAPTER 3
FINALLY THE FINALS

The Mystics finished the 2018 regular season with a strong 22–12 record and aimed to compete for a championship. Washington had never made it to the WNBA Finals. After defeating the Los Angeles Sparks in their first playoff matchup, the Mystics faced the Atlanta Dream. The winner would go on to play for the title in the Finals.

The teams split the first four games of the series, each winning two. The fifth and final game was close. In the fourth quarter, the teams each took the lead at different points. Mystics rookie guard Ariel Atkins hit two free throws with just over a minute left in the game to put Washington up 82–76.

Ariel Atkins (*left*) dribbles past Atlanta Dream defender Brittney Sykes (*right*) during the 2018 playoffs.

About 30 seconds later, the Dream's Alex Bentley made a long three-point shot to cut the Mystics' lead to 82–79. Suddenly, the game's outcome was in question again. After Atlanta's defense stopped the Mystics, the Dream's Tiffany Hayes made a basket. The Mystics' six-point lead was down to one.

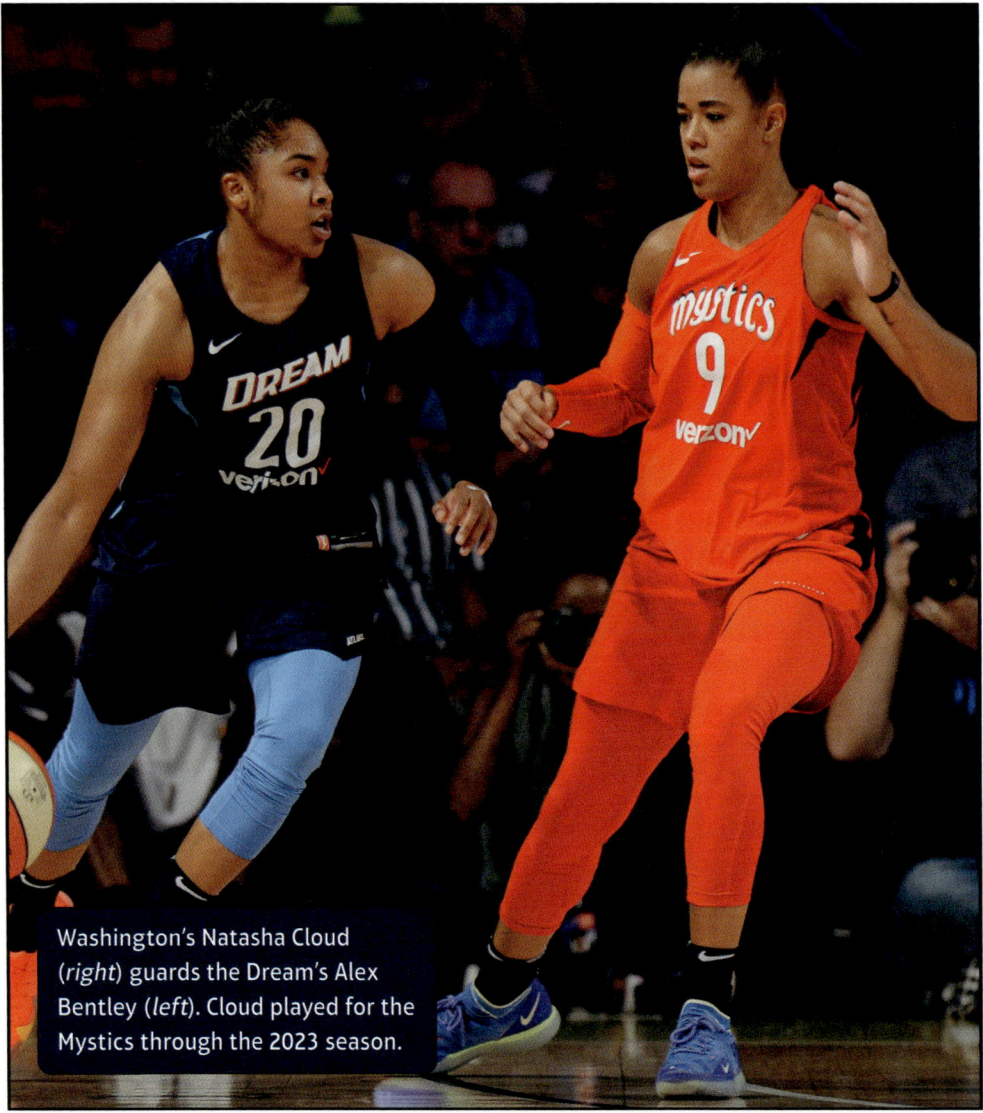

Washington's Natasha Cloud (*right*) guards the Dream's Alex Bentley (*left*). Cloud played for the Mystics through the 2023 season.

Elena Delle Donne started all 136 games she played in for the Mystics. She scored 2,551 points in her six seasons in Washington.

With time running down, the Dream fouled Delle Donne to stop the clock. She hit two free throws with 11.5 seconds left. The Mystics led 84–81. All that stood between them and their first trip to the WNBA Finals was one defensive stop.

HOOPS SCOOP

Alana Beard is the team's all-time leader with 364 steals.

Alana Beard (*center*) played six seasons for the Mystics before injuries paused her playing career. After she recovered, she played eight more seasons with the Los Angeles Sparks.

Dream star Tiffany Hayes dribbled outside the three-point line. She went around Mystics guard Natasha Cloud. Mystics forward LaToya Sanders charged at Hayes to stop her from taking an open shot. With Sanders' arm outstretched, Hayes jumped back and shot a three-pointer that could tie the game. But the ball fell far short of the rim and went out of bounds. Moments later, time expired and the Mystics won the game. They were heading to the WNBA Finals for the first time.

Although they didn't win the WNBA championship, 2018 is one of the best seasons in Mystics history.

Ariel Atkins grabbed 40 or more steals in five of her first seven seasons with the Mystics.

CHAPTER 4
A NEW START

The 2022 season was the last for record-setting coach Mike Thibault. He left coaching and became the team's general manager. His son, Eric Thibault, had been an assistant coach with the team from 2013 to 2022. He took over for his father as the team's head coach in 2023.

In 2023, after six seasons in Washington, Elena Delle Donne played her last game for the Mystics. Both Mike and Eric Thibault parted ways with the Mystics at the end of the 2024 season. Although it was the end of an era for the team, they were ready for a new one to start.

The departures of key player Elena Delle Donne (*left*) and coach Eric Thibault (*right*) meant big changes were in store for the Mystics.

Many skilled players remained on the team's roster after Delle Donne left the Mystics. Guard Ariel Atkins is the team's all-time leader in three-pointers. She also ranks second in steals, third in assists, and third in points. The two-time All-Star has played her entire career in Washington and took over for Delle Donne as the team's top scorer. Before an injury forced her to miss part of the 2024 season, guard Brittney Sykes earned a place on the 2023 WNBA All-Defensive Team.

Interest in the WNBA has never been higher. Exciting young stars, including Angel Reese of the Chicago Sky and Caitlin Clark of the Indiana Fever, mean more people than ever are watching. Fans in Washington, DC, are eager to see their Mystics compete for another WNBA title.

Brittney Sykes (*left*) blocks a shot by the Seattle Storm's Victoria Vivians (*right*) during a 2024 game.

Washington's Karlie Samuelson (*right*) guards the Fever's Caitlin Clark (*left*) in a 2024 game. Clark and other talented young players sparked a new interest in the WNBA for basketball fans.

GLOSSARY

All-Star: a player chosen as one of the best in league to compete in a game against other top players

assist: a pass that leads directly to a basket

expansion team: a team added to an existing sports league

free throw: an open shot taken from behind a set line after a foul by an opponent

rebound: when a player grabs and controls the ball after a missed shot

rookie: a first-year player

roster: a list of players on a team

title: championship

WNBA Draft: when WNBA teams take turns choosing new players

LEARN MORE

Doeden, Matt. *G.O.A.T. Women's Basketball Teams.* Minneapolis: Lerner Publications, 2021.

Mahoney, Brian. *GOATs of Basketball.* Minneapolis: Abdo Publishing, 2022.

Washington Mystics
https://mystics.wnba.com/

Whiting, Jim. *The Story of the Washington Mystics.* Mankato, MN: Creative Education and Creative Paperbacks, 2024.

WNBA
https://www.wnba.com/

Women's National Basketball Association Facts for Kids
https://kids.kiddle.co/Women%27s_National_Basketball_Association

INDEX

Atkins, Ariel, 5, 21, 28

Beard, Alana, 16
Bentley, Alex, 22

Cloud, Natasha, 25

Delle Donne, Elena, 5–6, 12, 18, 23, 27–28

Entertainment and Sports Arena, 9

Holdsclaw, Chamique, 10, 15

Langhorne, Crystal, 17

Meesseman, Emma, 12

Thibault, Eric, 27
Thibault, Mike, 17, 27

WNBA Draft, 10, 15–16
WNBA Finals, 5, 11, 21, 23, 25

PHOTO ACKNOWLEDGMENTS

Image credits: G Flume/Getty Images, p.4; Katherine Frey/The Washington Post/Getty Images, p.6; G Flume/Getty Images, p.7; Ezra Shaw/Getty Images, p.8; Patrick Smith/Getty Images, p. 9; G Flume/Getty Images, p.10; Otto Gruele Jr/Allsport/Getty Images, p.11; Tony Quinn/Icon Sportswire/Corbis/Getty Images, p.12; Michael A. McCoy/Getty Images, p.13; Doug Pensinger/Allsport/Getty Images, p.14; Preston Keres/The Washington Post/Getty Images, p.15; Joel Richardson/The Washington Post/Getty Images, p.16; Craig Hudson/The Washington Post/Getty Images, p.17; Scott Taetsch/Getty Images, p.18; Tony Quinn/Icon Sportswire/Getty Images, p.19; Rich von Biberstein/Icon Sportswire/Getty Images, p.20; Rich von Biberstein/Icon Sportswire/Getty Images, p.21; Rich von Biberstein/Icon Sportswire/Getty Images, p.22; Rich von Biberstein/Icon Sportswire/Getty Images, p.23; Joel Richardson/The Washington Post/Getty Images, p.24; Katherine Frey/The Washington Post/Getty Images, p.25; Chris Coduto/Getty Images, p.26; M. Anthony Nesmith/Icon Sportswire/Getty Images, p.27; Scott Taetsch/Getty Images, p.28; G. Flume/Getty Images, p. 29

Cover: Rich von Biberstein/Icon Sportswire DKB/Icon Sportswire/Newscom